So Speaks My Sea

So Speaks My Sea

Nature
and the
Soul

Theta Burke

Delafield Press   Suttons Bay, Michigan 49682

ISBN: 0-916872-10-6
Library of Congress Catalog Card Number: 95-92683
Printed in the United States of America

To Our Universe:

I love you, Sun
and moon and stars
and land and trees and sea
I love you, Earth
for all you are
and what you speak to me.

So Speaks My Sea

Nature
and the
Soul

1.

Please keep the coffee hot tonight
I'm standing watch, you know,
for the sea and I
need time to speak
      of things concerning the soul.

2.

Tonight
the still gray of the sky and sea
blend
And a filmy moon's pale glow
adds a ghostly air

Should a shadowy ship
            from some yesteryear
glide silently into view
I should not be surprised

It is that kind of night.

3.

Ah, the truth I see in Nature
a truth that each soul seeks
a truth that is the outward expression
of the inward beauty of each

Becoming aware of all that's given
speaks well the growth of the soul
The inner seeks the outer
so the two become a whole

       Beauty and love and language
       help each to know the other
       As each one learns expression
       the spirit blends them all together.

4.

I look out from the rocky coast
to the great waves
      and to the gentle ones
And I listen

And I hear the sea say to me:
I am glad you are here
I have known of your need for me
and I have sent my messages
I knew you would come
      and I have waited

Now you will learn my many moods
Hear all my sounds
And I will share with you
      my secrets
      and my strength
      and my foreverness.

5.

Different light
different depth
     make different colors
shown by the sea

Different love
different knowledge
     cause different responses
shown by me.

6.

The breezes stir
the branches nod
And I'm reminded
who is God.

7.

The waves as they wash against the shore
have a timeless, surging rhythm
in gentle laps or crashing roars
according to the power the sea has given

What might it be about the sea
that speaks so well to my soul
What causes the peace I come to feel
as I watch its eternal flow

    Perhaps it speaks to me of life
    and all the parts thereof
    as I see the waves come rolling in
    and watch them as they go

Returning to that from whence they came
they start their journey o'er
to return again in another time
in gentle laps or crashing roars
    And out to sea again.

8.

A strong sea breeze blows through your hair
as you stand with your hand on the helm
of a special ship that's called Yourself
and you pray that you steer her well

That you study the course you take her on
learn the waters shallow and deep
be ready whatever the weather
the vigil that's yours to keep

> That you learn the winds that fill her sails
> and direct them as you need
> to reach what port you're headed for
> embrace the word Believe

When the winds are low and her movement slow
and the rations are but few
may you trust in that
which built your ship
have faith it will see you through.

9.

The remaining fragments of ice
in the warming blue water
said in some alarm to each other:
What's happening to us −
we're all disappearing!

And the sea replied:
Fear not
Only your form is changing
You are but returning to that
from whence you came.

10.

The waves come into every shore
as though that shore belonged to them
and that's how it is with all the sea
where there be a shore
   that beckons them

And Love's a sea for all the world
and every soul a shore
and every wave of love that comes
says there is always more.

11.

When the wind blows strong
and the trees bend down
when the waves are whipped about
I'm aware of the power
    that Nature speaks
as I watch and hear from my sturdy house

I know should Nature speak her strength
my house could fall like straw
but I feel at one with what she is
and feel no fear at all

    For Love is one with Nature
    Love can still the storming sea
    And midst whatever nature shows
    Love will care for me.

12.

A thirst to be by the sea have I
when I am far away
and I miss the things it has to say
though Nature speaks in other ways

So I carry the sights and sounds inside
like the love I feel for a friend
like memories that give me comfort
when I cannot see my friend.

13.

A mountain
reaching toward the sky
lifts my spirit
and points me heavenward

And the sea
beckons me to regions
beyond myself
and to greater depths.

14.

No place else I'd rather be
than in my house beside the sea
at peace with what my world has shown
at peace with what my soul has known.

15.

I never cared much for all blue skies
I like some fluffy clouds about
or even the dark and stormy ones
that shut the blue skies out

      Clouds add dimension to the sky
      and I guess life's like that, too
      If there weren't some things to overcome
      how would we learn what we could do

So we take the clouds however they be
from fluffy white to stormy gray
and know the sun is back of them all
with Love the sun that warms life's way.

16.

On a ship I came a'sailing
from a World we've never seen
And that, my friends, might just explain
why I love the sea

Now I don't remember much about
that Land from which I came
But things are felt from deep inside
that speak of something I can't name

And I think you know just what I mean
for you have felt the same –
those far-back stirrings once in a while
that your mind can't quite explain

I think our souls know an ancient truth
from which we sometimes stray afar
of a special mission we have in life
to *learn* and *be* the things we are

And coming to that particular truth
brings all the peace we need to know
It puts our life on its special course
that takes us where we need to go
        And safely to whatever Shore.

17.

Action and stillness
        are as the ebb and flow
of the sea.

Stillness is not inaction
It is *internal* action.

18.

It's not a different sky I see
from where I'm standing now
than the sky I watched long years ago
when I would wonder when and how

The stars, the moon, the sun and wind
and the earth I've trod upon
all have listened to my dreams
and helped me learn to sing my song

And I pray that I shall ever listen
to all the things they say to me
Stay quiet enough that I may hear
messages whispered by the breeze.

19.

Are not the shadows
        but a confirmation
of the sun?

20.

I feel a special excitement
       as I watch the spring earth
being turned by a plow

It speaks the marriage
of Man's efforts and Nature's laws
       which can bring forth
any harvest.

21.

Early spring and baby leaves
just starting to come out
Nature giving exciting examples
of what she's all about

Spring's a special child of Nature
just waking from her sleep
speaking life's beginnings
sowing seeds which fall shall reap

Her arrival always brings us hope
as she speaks of things to come
body and spirit feel renewed
by the warming energy of her sun

And spring grows into summer
long warm "becoming" days
preparing for the harvesting
which fall shall bring our way

And fall will still remember
what started what it is
and will show its appreciation
by a colorful show and harvest bread

Winter's the quiet and resting time
with snow that's Nature's coverlet
protecting what will live again
a time of peace and quiet content

So on and on the seasons go
each speaking Nature's way
in different dress and different voice
each one has its say.

22.

The forest now is thinned by years
the trees don't stand so thick and tall
But love has walked among them
and love has given all

       And the memories give the forest life
       from love that never dies
       Memories leave a golden glow
       speaking still of what was known

Yes, twilight now will speak its quiet
to a soul who's known the sun
And memories of the love that's been
bring peace with the night to come.

23.

Say three brown leaves:
We hung on tight
the winter long
through quiet snow
      and blowing storms

But with the silent
      push of spring
we'll be replaced
by leaves of green.

24.

Early Leelanau April
Bare cherry tree limbs
      becoming pregnantly pink –
anticipating.

25.

In Defense of the Dandelion:
He's such a hearty fellow
who comes along each spring
to add a bit of color
he doesn't really hurt a thing

But it seems that some don't like him
they try to kill him off
but the breezes help him propogate
as they lift his seeds aloft

And I think no matter what we do
he'll always find a way
to speak the message he has to give
He likes what he has to say!

26.

One night I saw a special star
one I'd never seen
twinkling there against the night
starbright – then red then green

       I looked another night to see
       if I could find my star
       but it was nowhere in the sky
       and I pondered my special star

Would it come another time
or was it gone forever
Yet it would stay within my mind
a special star forever.

27.

Now East is West
     and West is East
It depends on where we stand
And we need keep
     this truth in mind
as we survey the state of man

For if I were able to follow the sun
to where the West does end
I'd go with it in a circle
to where the East begins.

28.

I love the sun as it rises and sets
and the moon and the stars and the sky
and the hills and trees and oceans and lakes
But what's inside makes me know why

The sense of awareness of all that *is*
is a wealth that can't be told
a treasure ever with us
not a thing to be bought or sold.

29.

Father Love and Mother Nature
speak the wisdom of all time
say whatever needs be said
hold the truths we seek to find

We need to look from whence we came
to find out who we are
and if Love and Nature born'd us
no place we dream can be too far

       Our guides are written on Nature's face
       we need not look another place
       Nature and Love go hand in hand
       one only shows what the other has planned.

30.

Autumn Scandal
Goodness me
I am distressed
as I watch the trees
     becoming undressed!

31.

I gazed upon
my sea of blue
and I thought that I
would bring to you
a bucket of blue

I dipped my
little bucket in
I looked – and then
I dipped again.

And now this question
I bring to you –
Whatever happened
to the blue?

32.

September sun moves a bit to the South
and smiles a gentle warmth
looking on the harvest work
which he with earth and man
    brought forth

He'll keep on going slowly South
giving winter its resting time
The Southern tropics he'll favor then
to begin *their* growing times

    But he'll not hide his face from us
    though his warmth be far away
    And when there's sunlight on the snow
    we can hear him say:

I'll be back to warm your earth
before it's time to sow your seeds
Fear not – I am ever knowing
I am mindful of your needs.

33.

The life of a leaf
      from its tiny bud
to a deep rich glowing bronze
is a study in art
      and a lesson in faith
as I watch what can become.

34.

If you would send a thought to me
just tell it to a star
It will beam your message to me
from whatever place you are

Or speak it to a fluffy cloud
that rides upon the wind
It will see that I shall hear
any message you might send

And if you be far, far away
perhaps across the sea
The waves that travel from shore to shore
will bring your love to me

There's not a way to get beyond
the reach of love that's felt
And any time that love is sent
all of Nature waits to tell.

35.

I like to travel country roads
away from the glare of city lights
where the dark and the stars and the friendly moon
let night still be the way I like

The stillness of the countryside
and the lights from the farmhouse windows
take me back to other years
times I like to remember

Where my soul had time to listen
to absorb from Nature's store
messages that the quiet spoke
and the time to learn there was always more

Not a need was there to hasten
in gathering to myself
all the things my soul might need
for they were waiting inside my Self.

36.

Spoke a rose
I heard today
No words it needed
to convey
   Its Essence told
   what it could not say.

37.

The river goes
as the river flows
It chooses not its way
Not more can we
     direct the course
that our affections say

Sometimes the flood
sometimes the drought
which causes joy or pain
But the river goes
     as the river flows
not counting loss or gain.

38.

The sun has spoken much to me
of what I know of life
from its rising in the morning
till I see it set at night

I watch it on its journey
and I see some things it causes
Its warmth and light it gives to all
not basing its giving on who's deserving

And when its face is covered by clouds
I know it's still up there
Whatever things I need of it
are filtered through the air

Its strength is felt when it's not in sight
Love's message is the same
And all the truths of life are ours
as our hearts can learn their names.

39.

Sleepy, lazy summer days
when there's hardly a breeze that stirs
and the creak of the chains
    on the old porch swing
is mostly the sound that's heard

Some birds that chirp in the full green trees
the crow of the rooster
    across the way
the drone of the tractor out in the fields
Sounds of summer days.

40.

The creativity that nature shows
is a pattern that all can learn
We show it each
        in our special way
as our hearts learn
how to discern.

41.

Openness
      desert
      sea
      sky and
love.

42.

Butterflies and sunshine
balmy breezes brush my brow
springtime speaking new beginnings
love and nature showing how

Speaking softly to my spirit
of the things that I need know
for my journey of the moment
or traveling toward a farther goal

Ah, there's power in that message
strength to ever lift my heart
with soft and understanding silence
when I'm weary – slow to start

Yes, there's purpose in my Being
beyond a way that I may see
And when I doubt I need remember
it's built inside where the spirit sees.

43.

What will you do with no mountain to climb
or a thing that needs be done
when it seems that life's just passing
toward the setting sun

You've reached some goals you set for yourself
and you feel you've done right well
But it's restless you are as you look about
and you search for a higher grail

Is it time, perhaps, to stop and think
to ask what the soul might need
Perhaps some dreams have lost their way
and those are still the ones you seek

> Be still – and quiet the outer din
> Each soul must search its own
> So give it time that it may know
> And ascend its proper throne.

44.

When I am tired and weary
with the hurts of the world
      puppies
      and kittens
      and skies at sunset
can make me smile.

45.

I would not bridle you, Dreams of mine
I would follow you in my Fancy
        where'er you'd take me
and be grateful
        for the experiences
you bring to my Imaginations

And when great Hope
accompanies some of you
I must know also
that Pain may sometimes pierce me
        through your delay or change

But to restrain you
would not allow the possibility
        for the Joy
which also can come through your Fulfillment

Yes, I will follow you,
    Dreams of mine
And through your freedom
I shall learn my own.

46.

So often
those things we fear
are as harmless to us
     as are we
to the birds
     who fly away
when we pass near the feeder
     we have provided for them.

47.

Giving is like a river
that takes its gifts from little streams
and ever carries them onward
to give where'er might be a need

And the river goes on to its ocean
where the sun and sea and wind cause rain
to return to earth from whence it came
and the giving cycle starts again

If we but learn from Nature
we'll know a better way of giving
and paying heed to all her ways
will teach a better way of living.

48.

Said the Bird to the Frog
You live in a bog
How can you stand it there
Oh, said the Frog,
I was made for the bog
Just how do *you*
      fly in the air?

49.

Leelanau moon
      over hills
soft with cherry blossoms
casts its pale beams
      on hushed twilight waters

And I wonder
that there need be reason
for anything but peace.

50.

Winter fog slowly settles
over the earth
like a warm soft blanket
tucking Nature in.

51.

We know that *gardens* require
    cultivation and patience
But too often we forget to apply
    this understanding
to our own life
and relationships.

52.

I saw this morn
the sun being born
and I saw
     a bird on the wing
I heard the sound
of the sea coming in –
Now don't I have reason to sing!

53.

Be not dismayed
when your external behavior
        falls short
of your internal vision

Our growing
is not a steady incline
but a more attractive terrain
        of hills and valleys

And our acceptance
        of our present state
allows growth
at whatever level.

54.

Do you have time to come for a walk
through the wood or down by the sea
If you would come
      we need not speak
for our souls need time to see

Our talking might frighten the spirits
who'd share with us their way
And as we walk and listen
we'll hear what words could never say

Of course, we must walk very slowly
there's much to see and hear
and it may take a while
      for our spirits
to become acquainted with the spirits there

With time for the quiet to o'ertake us
as we shed our garments of care
away from the world we come to ourselves
partake of the peace
that is waiting there

A peace so great
that it may bring a tear
to a soul who has thirsted long
like a lover home to his loved one
And the stillness becomes a song.

55.

I look out at the morning
and see the rising sun
and though the stars have disappeared
it doesn't mean they're gone

Sunshine and the light of day
can make a beautiful sight
but a special kind of beauty
can only be seen at night

Some things that show in darkness
shadows of night and the stars and moon
speak a quietness to the soul
have a message all their own.

56.

The tree stood
tall and strong.
Some saw the ridges of its bark
      the veins of its leaves.
Others saw only its outline.

57.

I bend
  with the winds
while my roots
  grow strong
reach as deep
  as the need
when love is my song.

58.

The shells that rest
      on the shores of the sea
the stars above that shine on me
the wind, the rain, the moon and sun
say to me I'm not alone

      The mountains speak
            their strength to me
      saying they shall ever be
      And I watch the rivers
            continue to flow
      speaking life I've learned to know

As Nature speaks to me her way
I learn to hear what love would say
How can I ever be alone
with Love and Nature as my home.

59.

Our intellectual awareness
      can be an ocean
in which we drown
when it is separated
      from our emotional involvement
and experiential interaction
with our environment.

60.

Does a caterpillar know
      that interacting
with a mulberry leaf
can produce silk

Cannot we, then, believe
      that our own interactions
can accomplish similar wonders
perhaps never known to us.

61.

I love the quiet darkening
    of the sky
before a storm
a dimming of the stage lights
    before lightning parts the curtain
on one of Nature's spectacular performances
And the thunder applauds.

62.

We like it in the wintertime
my little stove and I
I sit beside with pen and pad
while he winks a glowing eye

We like it in the morning dark
when all our world is still
no sound intrudes save the crackling log
and the snow lies soft
     on the window sill.

63.

Unfold, little rose
Thy beauty
      in time
will only increase

Because I said yesterday
      I like you as you are,
thou needst not fear
to *become.*

64.

I think there truly is a way
for man to meet his every need
Nature holds for us the answers
as we but learn to see

When we survey the way we've come
as we have searched her ways
can there really be a doubt
of all the wisdom she can say

      She gives to us the clues we need
      and a few there are who see
      who harness some of her limitless power
      to cause some wondrous things to be.

65.

Man does not *tame* Nature

By learning and responding
    to her laws
there develops a relationship
where each becomes the richer
    through constructive interaction.

66.

I have known the sun
that has shown on every man
    the stars and seas and skies and trees
and the beauty of the land

I walk the paths of ages past
and see from whence I came
    And what's been known by any man
I can know the same

For love – the central force of life
is mine to draw upon
    As I learn to assimilate and share
I know what's needed shall be done

    There's nothing new that we can learn
        of love
    which others haven't known
    But life is learning how to cause
    those truths to be our own.

67.

We look within
      and look beyond
the sources that are ours
and know what efforts
      that we spend
are matched by a greater power.